Cover image and rear cover photo © copyright (2018) Peter Eustace
Cover layout adviser Pascale Gouverneur MA

Editing, layout and typesetting; © copyright (2018) Dr. Alan Corkish

erbacce-press publications Liverpool UK 2018

erbacce-press.com
ISBN: 978-1-912455-05-8

Peter Eustace has published two books of poems in English and Italian (*Vistas*, 2006, and *Weathering*, 2010) and an English-only pamphlet (*Brink*, 2009) with *erbacce press*, Liverpool. He has been a guest at the Valpolicella, Verona, Monte Baldo and Nogara poetry festivals (Italy), as well as the Small Press Day/10th anniversary of the UNESCO World Academy of Poetry in Verona. He was the featured poet in issue 45 of *erbacce* magazine (June 2016) and an invited poet in the 50th issue of *erbacce*. Other poems have appeared on-line and in print (*Carillon, Borderlines, Ink, Sweat and Tears, Equinox, The French Literary Review, Obsessed with Pipework, The Bow-Wow Shop, Epicentre, Trespass*). Two of his poems opened the *Carillon* Ten Forward anthology.

Peter lives in Verona, Italy.

For Tina

Index:

SIGHTING LAND

The rugged wind harangues the sails, tinkles the night-watch bells - tricks
Recalling the creaky gate at home I always meant to fix
After attending to the livestock and the hayricks.

Prow-kicked spray, like sand-galloping horses,
Plummets my memory back to impossible moons on known shores
Many months behind us, ceaselessly seeking, among the nightmares,

Boundless new lands to populate with our wares, our fears.

COME IN NUMBER NINE ...

Your time is up.
But you knew that
From the outset,
Didn't you? Of course.
Yet like everyone else
You preferred to ignore
The countdown – there
Were other things to do,
Other things to pretend
Would not happen,
The nightmares, the
Occasional inkling there
Might be happiness,
The generalised realisation
That there isn't.
Duty, the usual convictions
Behind those guilt-making
Beliefs so hard to believe
When the wrong questions
Are asked and even
Wronger answers given.
Life, I suppose.
Come in number nine.

PLODDING ON

I've given up gambols
And bowl off a shorter run-up.
I have become my own fossil,
The past a buried antiquity
Popping out of memory's suitcases
Unexpectedly exhumed
Yet immediately packed away again.
Bits of litter may be left over.

HERE AND NOW
"Siamo qui, siamo soli" Vasco Rossi

We are here, we are on our own.
We shall not stay all that long –
Time enough, perhaps, to atone
For being here in the first place.

Then we'll be gone without trace
Like the blurred lyrics of a song
Once popular fallen into disgrace.
A stumble at the final furlong.

ABERFAN

I remember the news that day
When the slag-mountain worked loose
By rain slumped down on the school
I was young enough to be at myself.

I felt my nostrils fill with liquefied
Coal dust, the black air clogging
My throat, the sting in the eyes;
Huge gasps hauling at air only

Took in more grit; the pounding
In the ears, the lung-bursting gulps
And long silence. I was supposed
Not to be old enough to understand.

LOST AND FOUND

Queuing for the lost and found
We find it's mostly lost,
That self-destruction attracts
The star-seeking moth
Infuriated by the kitchen
Light bulb. A kind of obsessed
Determination to do the wrong thing.
Our tragedy lies in taking our tragedy
Too seriously, pressing buttons
At random to soothe the threatened
Being in a vain hope of finding
The right yet improbable combination.

THE BIG POEM

This is the very big poem.
It has a lot to say.
It has been a long time
In the making.
A lifetime, to tell the truth.
It's about slick midnights
And grimly boring afternoons.
It might mention how greed
And violence write history.
It may tell how enduring landscapes
Become disrupted. There will be room
For Sunday drunks, squandering
The pursuit of happiness as they
Dawdle along the paper chase.
There will be no eye-catching words.
Then again, I may prefer
To gaze at those pot-bellied clouds
In limp-home mode dumping stray
Raindrops that squabble with the air's
Quibbling breeze. There may be
Standing room only for the last few lines,
Hoping they might at last rhyme.

IN MEMORIAM

Time's perfected, cruel tricks -
Seeming to stand still
Only the flywheel
Always whirrs, whizzes
Behind the glass:
You grew old faster
Than us, and we did not
Have the chance to say goodbye.

GAPS

This is what a poem looks like:
Some scribble here and there
And too much or too little white space.
Gaps everywhere surrounding
Occasional snippets of second-hand
Wisdom, half-truths half-understood,
Platitudes and tautology. Endlessly.
A constant collection of things
To sift through again and again
Kept as heirloom ballast for someone
Else to throw away at other times
That will never come for us. We hang
On to knickknacks: they are easier
On the heart than our intangible losses.

There are so many gaps, empty crevices,
Spaces that widen into eroded voids
And vacuums, black holes in the pit
Of the stomach where the spirit sinks,
Implodes. The difference between
What's said and what's meant, the sayer's
And the hearer's versions, incessantly building
Hand-me-downs of rickety awareness
Shuffling, fluttering, becoming worn out
Or merely lost under new piles of cast-offs.
Things that refuse to be pinned down,
Churning, turning sour, growing mould.
The lists of what we never did, the hours
Wasted getting it all wrong again.

Groping with the insignificant magnitude
Of boundaries keeping us apart in permanent
Communion. The wheedle and the whine
Simmering into raging argument, spilling over,
Rioting purposelessly. Fraught stars like
A million pinhole cameras scrutinise us,
Capturing snapshots of cosmic nothingness.
Outrage bungles its syllables, brute force
Hammering perverse silence. We cannot allay
These grieving times, inuring hearts and minds
To suffering, downtrodden and mangled.
Noise quietens. The air tingles with remnants
Of anger, stumbling like pebbles in a stream
Yearning for smoothness, peace from guilt.

Shyly ashamed, we rely on duplicitous landmarks.
Power whittles away at the soul's resistance
To the greedy horror a gleeful minority
Practices with dissolute piety on the rest of us
Till we even beg for our own downfall. Dereliction.
A self-abhorrent, habitual, self-constructed prison
Of dishonesty, half-truths, untruths and no truths at all.
Blind eyes turned over and over as we accelerate
To join the queue determined to get a bigger one next time.
Our prescriptions and our pills dutifully taken,
Our obedience to laws made by law-breakers,
We celebrate the ephemeral, taking glamour seriously;
Hoodwinked, deceived, we let them create
And defend compassionless privilege.

Life-searches shuffle, intact but bottomed out,
Padlocked and rusted with no magic words
To shear the chains, ease the stricken memory.
Wreck wreaked world. Fighting it out with
Fickle gods, squeezing intentions into
Components gmo-ing the supernatural.
A malingering. Apparently unperturbed,
Stillness returns, settles back much as before.
A storm snorts away into the distance.
Its air shifts the clouds' dying turbulence
Like a broomstick reminding us of mortality
Hidden in our interstitial depths. The mind
And its un-implementable providence
Is scuttled on its way to the breaker's yard.

Women at the looms pumping the shuttle's
Foot pedals, seated in just that skewwhiff way
That brought them to multiple orgasm
Day-long, turning drudging hours into
Something half-tolerable. They went home
Exhausted to exhausted men black with coal
Keen only for a bite to eat and beer.
Their snuff-punctuated, dull conversations
Hailed up the alleys and backyards strung with
Washing lines across the outside loos' slate roofs.
Slate that glimmered in the half-light
After dark rain – a sheen of almost-beauty –
Piling up over the crooked railway bridge
Where the pub huddled its cheap dreams

And the one-time manor house,
Its light-tax-avoiding bricked-up windows
Like badly healed wounds. Borrowed memories:
Kids play on a broken swing by the remains
Of an Anderson shelter. The attempted vegetable
Plot has gone to seed just like the gardener's
Attempted, thwarted life. Those boys, brothers,
Daring the night in half-lit doorways determined
To watch the searchlights and listen for the squeal
Of falling bombs, estimating where tomorrow
They would find the gap like a lost tooth
In the next street's lined-up terraced slums,
The rubble and the mourning.
Fallen arches, fallen angels, fallen idols.

Grunting blood mutters,
Niggles at the tinkering mind.
Breaches and infringements implode
In incomprehensible havoc that
Churns a kind of exile in the gap
Between desire and reality,
A getting used to (even hoping for)
Unhappiness while learning
To do without bandages, realising
That our cures do not always heal.
Singing praises of destructive gods,
Wealth explains – and justifies – poverty.
Floundering in the shallows, life is its
Smatterings, its scowls, its scrawls.

The most memorable thing is how little
There really is to recall: grey streets
Slouching their way squeezed between
Tiny, packed greyer houses pumping
Grim smoke out of dirty chimneys
Into bald skies that always seemed ready
To pour over washing always hung out
To dry that rarely did. Boys duck-arsing
Hand-me-round cigarettes only to cough
Their guts up and feel sick. They scuffed
Their shoes home to the ritual thick ear
And thin-sliced bread spread even more
Thinly with jam before going to bed
With chilblains wheezing to sleep.

SALVAGE

"Shepherds, peasants, craftsmen, merchants, inn-keepers,
priests, prostitutes – all the ingredients needed to found
a city." Giuseppe Antonelli - *The History of Ancient Rome,
from the Origins to the End of the Republic*

Evidently, they had hopes for you,
Romulus Augustus, consummately destined
To bring two beginnings to one end.

You were too young to understand
The peepshow of history, where
What is past and what's impending

Flickered towards your future,
Centuries compressed into
Fraught moments when the mob

At last had its heyday.
Your end before you could begin
Had long been going on unawares.

Did your daunted mind slip
Back to that grubby, ordinary start –
The safe ford, safe hills, kidnapped

Women, the short, efficient sword
And mastery of pragmatism –
Or did history's bickering get

In the way as it happened around you?
You did not have time enough
To perfect your own expertise

In treachery and intrigue
Yet youth and ineptitude were,
Of course, your salvation, your wreck

Left for salvage not quite forgotten,
As power took new guises,
Wore a different purple.

JUMBLE SALE

I am my own fossil,
My many lives buried
Beneath oceans of history,
Compacted, compressed.

Only inklings, exercises
In indifference
And the certainty that
Nothing is certain.

Wisdom ought to be
A capacity for surprise,
Astonishment, a kind
Of temporary dying

Struggling for breath,
Resurfacing, restarting ...
A hinted knowledge
Of possible futures.

The past cranks up
Its heritage of antiques,

Buried and forgotten,
Sometimes re-exhumed

Crusted with time's neglect.
Bits of self that
Won't let us shut
Memory's suitcase.

Days turn dormant,
Recede imperceptibly
Into the past:
They come and go, like

These words where
I have lived my life,
Turning their backs
At times, like a lover

Spurned, or bursting banks
Incomprehensibly.
Words so easily become
Uninhabitable.

POLES APART

"Proceed trustfully, I shew the way" Epigraph from:
Trade Mark London, The Story of Francis Barker
& Son - Compass and Scientific Instrument Makers
- Paul Crespel

Our apparently reliable instruments
        Brought us here,
Where we no longer have any sense
        Of where we are going, nor even
Where we are or where we came from.

There are infinite, interminable ways
        Of going in the opposite direction
But only one way out, pulled to
        Another absolute extreme.
The compass has dipped

To its own Nirvana, is stuck,
        Unable to veer or point
To a way we should take –
        Finding its own home at last,
It only tells us we are lost.

Confused, we have to get to know
        Our own fallibility –
What we think we understand
        Changes, needs adjusting:
Landmarks can be deceptive, readings

Untrustworthy. All deviations must be
        Accounted for, all declinations –
We can put no faith in our certainties:
        Things drift, are dragged off track,
Affected by local discrepancies.

Here, at one of the countless
        Mid-points of infinity, it
Is like Zeno's stone never reaching ground
        Or prime numbers splitting
Eternally into incontrollable fractions.

DILEMMA

It's fucking hot inside a tank,
Working skid-steer joysticks
In a radio-controlled helmet
And all that other war-gear

Until some young office prat
Tie-less in a white shirt
Holding a black briefcase
Decides to get in the way.

I mean, he was unarmed.
Right? I was under orders,
Of course, on duty,
And definitely trained to kill –

Kill our enemies who
Didn't materialise here,
In the people's square
Where both of us wordlessly

And ultimately prepared
For the obedient firing squad.

STORM

Inhospitable paradise.
I thought I knew you,
That you knew me,
Till your ancient eyes
Suddenly

Gouged another iced,
Hail-bouncing tempest
From deceptive skies
Indiscriminately
Scouring us,

Stranded. In the after-calm,
Nothing went on happening
Again as only nothing can -
Except your great psalm.

DOG-ROSE THICKET

Thorns grasp at the sky,
Take root in the clouds.

Wind-borne, animal-undigested
Seeds found this poor-soiled,
Weather-exposed limestone declivity,
Fortuitously carried from the dag-crowded,
Insect-attacked valley lower down

Where pollen-rich, nectar-less
Pinkishly-white flowers entice birds
And the red husks of vitaminic hips
Are whiskered in impenetrable bundles
Outlasting even the worst winter.

You were left to bramble
Only because you keep
The cows out of the pit.

CLINTS AND GRYKES

No water to drown in, wood enough
for gallows or earth for burials.

Strong drink metes the cold,
Soothes the soul's runnels
Till memory's swallow holes
Sink into forgotten histories

Of erratics, mind-boulders,
Glacial and hydrochloric.
Erosion. Getting old,
Greyly-eternal, in this
Dwarfing immensity.

THE DYING GAUL

We took the easy walk up Michelangelo's flattened
Steps into the square adorned around Mark Anthony
Riding history, stalked the banns for the concerned
And curious along the porticos and into the museum,

Summoning up the usual dull interest in collected,
Soulless things, trying not to admit the tedium
Of poor busts, cracked plates and faded canvas –
Till you drew us, Gaul, in your dying, life's blood

A torrent in your wound, your relinquishing throes
Of mortality propped on a flexing arm
As you sank into the silence of your death,
Chunked hair, flinched muscles, defiance

In your warrior eyes, the grimace, a last
Breath still pent up in your bursting chest.

HENRY ON A REASONABLE DAY

They married me off to my dead brother's wife -
The wrong-named Arthur who sweated to death at Ludlow.
Sad-old Catherine was mere diplomacy, our duty in life.

We tried. I'd expected to hunt, fuck and grow mellow
Irresponsibly - till the unwanted Crown stung belief
In that necessary heir; I told the Ambassador fellow

From Spain she was old, ugly, foreign and barren,
That surviving-Mary would never cope with my island,
That we simply had to find another solution.

I banished them all. Yet every now and then, even as Anne
Soothes my lust, I wish my Princess Dowager would send
Me music for the songs I write in contrition

For my wrongs with her forgiveness.
Only my wandering eyes already have this other empress.

HENRY ON A BAD DAY

"Three Kates and two Annes,
Two foreigners and a couple of maids.
A church changed and statesmen's
Lands taken with their heads.

What was duty was never love.
What, damn my father, could I ever prove?"

HISTORY

The long, endless process
Of getting things wrong
Again and again:

Beauty runs aground,
Becomes derelict as
Time obliterates its hopes

In constant betrayal.
Yet the search for it
Is our only redemption.

HERMIT

We strut this earth
With a fear of fear
And put five minutes
On the clock
To live safely by.

We would want our heartbeats
To be earthquakes,
Our faces divine deserts
With oases for eyes.
Yet we are only hermits.

REJECT

I am no longer suitable
For my intended purpose.
I need regular maintenance
And do not always
Respond to commands.
I consume too much.
I have become rough
At the edges, and worn
Smooth where I shouldn't be.
I have given you good service
But cheaper models are
Now available. I shall
Be sent for scrap, be
Recycled, and may even
Turn up again in something
Else you own. Be kind.

FOUNDRYMEN

Gulps of guffawing fumes billow in heaps,
Ceaselessly exploding as the furnace door
Is opened and shut, it's devil-red mouth
A gateway toing and froing infernal ingots
Of brass in moulds for ships' bells.
The whites of the eyes of the loin-clothed
Men glimmer starkly, almost menacingly,
In the hissing blackness. They douse themselves
With water, constantly, wear wet caps, wet towels
Wrapped around their necks, nodding rather than speaking.
They swing great mauls back and forth
To knock the air out of the castings,
Sweat and grime seeping deeply
Into every pore, tattooing every wrinkle.
The two of them fiendishly, rhythmically ferry
Molten metal, sand, rough-skinned casts,
In unspoken unison, swaying bare arms,
Bare, booted legs in implicit trust,
Wheezing softly as they hump their loads,
Knowing their coughs can only get worse.

THE COALMEN

When they were late coming to us,
They were already imbued with dust:
Smiles left frail, pale tracks in the black make-up
Of their faces, the whites of their eyes peering
All but ominously from under peaked caps,
Rags revealing scrawny white lines
Around their necks. They spat phlegm and oaths
As they heave-hoed the sacks off the lorry,
Bracing all-but double to their noisy boots
As they pounded their way up the steps to the
Coalhouse. Another heave and the load went
Crashing in, billowing fine black clouds
Like miniature thunderstorms.
They came and went in minutes, cascading
The innards of the earth into daydreams.

THE TEDDY BOYS

Crafty fags did the rounds
Passing from hand to hand,
Lips to lips for deep, melodramatic
Drags. A wet and spluttered
Puff betrayed jeered inexperience –
"So who duck-arsed it, then?" –
Setting off the foulest, vociferous
Swearing competitions and boasts
Of highly unlikely sexual prowess
Greeted by rude gestures and belly laughs.
Combs came out of back pockets
For quick flicks through quiffs
While belching. Wolf whistles
And farts. Boys being boys
Who sometimes became men.

ROCKETS

That boy, the only-child four houses
Up the street, only had rockets
On Bonfire Night. We had
To make do with Bengal matches,
Sparklers, bangers and Catherine wheels.
But he had the rockets. He didn't
Come penny-for-the-guying with us
Or build a bonfire in his own
Back garden or steal bits of wood
From council flat kids at the top of the road.
Just the rockets. A dozen, perhaps fifteen
Or even twenty. His Dad set them up
And let them off. He boasted
About them, how much they cost
And how much better they were
Than anything of ours.
I reckon, though, he really wanted
To light a banger's fuse with us
Than watch his old man
Playing at being a boy again.

THE SEWING BOX

It was left behind after her hasty heirs
Sold the place she'd called home for fifty years
Along with all kinds of other once-loved
Worthless things. A lifetime's trinkets.

She diligently collected buttons snipped
From worn-out shirts and threadbare overcoats,
Hooks and eyes and some foreign coins
Left over from church trips. Lengths

Of ribbon. There were no scribbled love-notes,
No photographs, no other items of endearment –
Only reels and reels of cotton, packets
With strands of wool and a pin cushion

Hedgehogged with far too many bent needles –
An inkling that even darned socks can be love.

SNOW HILL

A clattering rigmarole of light
Progressively diminishing into
A multitude of angular shafts
Catching glints of steel,
A wheeze of smoke and steam.
Locomotives chug like
Pent-up beasts resting
After combat, as another
Snigger of sunshine pierces
The blackened canopy
Of cast iron and glass
Crusted with decades of soot
And grime. Men like
Skittles strut in and out
Of shadows signalling orders
With swift hands and a rumpus
Of whistles. Asthmatic
Whooshes of steam and smoke
Erupt as engines gently draw long,
Slow, huge breaths at first
Like snorts of pain,
Then faster, deeper, insistent,
Building a strong, lulling
Rhythm as a train pulls out,
Stretching its joints like
A limbering athlete.
Noise peaks, then abides,
Leaving a counterfeit silence
Broken by incoherent calls,
Other carriages clanging
To an iron-on-iron standstill.
Resumption, ceaselessly.

THESE HANDS

These hands should
Cup pure water
For you to drink,
Shape into a shield
To protect you.

These hands should
Lift your spirit
When the world's
Misgivings and frivolities
Consume you.

These hands should take
Yours and lead
You to safe havens,
They should be strong
When you stumble.

These hands should bless
Your pain, build your roof
And grow your food,
Join yours in thanks,
In some kind of prayer.

These hands should be
A healing caress,
Wise and reassuring,
Guiding your way
Until you can go alone.

These hands, these
Faltering, incapable hands,
Should ask your
Forgiveness and
Share your pardon.

URBANICS

Town-smell: old chip-fat burning, melding with steam,
Burnt coffee, leftover veg moulding up scruffy alleys,
Confectionery nauseating the breeze on wrong-wind days,
Piss in not quite dark corners, half a bottle of cheap
Perfume the old hag sprinkles on everything within reach,
Car exhaust and smouldering electricals, rubber stench
First sticky, then brittle. Closed places stacked
With bits of mildew-furniture woodworm have feasted on
For years, barely intact until the last touch shatters them.
Two dozen farthings in a cracked Wedgewood dish, all worthless,
And a silver sixpence that might have once survived
A Christmas pudding. Yesterday's newspaper cut
Into squares and skewered on a nail in the outside loo
That was always cold and damp and dark even in high Summer.
Curtains thrown back to let daggering light pierce the darkness,
Catching floats of disturbed dust, hints of glass and metal,
Suddenly giving shape to smells of once-oiled appliances
Cooped up for years that will never work again.

SITTING DOWN TO BREAKFAST

*"The bundle of accident and incoherence
that sits down to breakfast"* – W.B. Yeats

Sleep, the great healer,
Doesn't always bring us peace
But torments unconscious hours
With mortality's crossed lines.

It is a dour pilgrimage,
A clattering rigmarole of dark voices
Up darker alleys… interstitial
Depths of imagination reminding

Us of the unarguable authority
Of death seen through improbable
Windows overlooking overgrown
Pastures. Compassion's providential

Salvation is scuppered, like notes
Of music turning into birds that
Abruptly fly away, leaving only
Silence and solitude. Learning

The ropes means tying knots…
Coming to terms with the magnitude
Of our insignificance over this ritual
Of tea, toast and marmalade.

WORDS

These words, little more than trinkets, piffle,
Trade in counterfeits with the soul
(Should there be one).
They stack loose change in separate piles
Hoping they might add up one day
To sums almost enough to pay
A bigger bill. A shambles, bric-à-brac,
Surreptitiously changing meanings

As time plunders and loots along
Its gaudy way, hooting from start to finish.
They strut, preposterously, gasp, grunt
And grapple with approximations
Stuffed into boxes that are too small
Or wallow in shallow waters
Or clatter against the bars of mindless cages.
Simpletons, yet our only hope.

An occasional monument mutters and natters
In memory's swamps. Words are alligators,
Prowling semi-submerged among
Neurons' mangrove roots, dense, impenetrable,
Repetitive, tarnished, unclear.
Some creatures learn their way around
Among the gaps, the misunderstandings,
Throwing words at the page

Hoping someone will catch the re-bound
And pass them on and even help them
Come home again with a new suit of clothes,
Walking sticks, walking frames, wheelchairs,
Provided the sparkle still glimmers there.
I tinker with the search engine.
It cranks up sometimes, spluttering, coughing.
It takes me places, like somewhere and nowhere.

MORE WORDS

(i)

Words strut like clumsy soldiers
On obedient parade grounds
Learning to march for no other reason
Than learning to march.

If only they would settle,
Become smooth and customary,
As reliable as the marble bollards
A thousand hands caress a thousand

Times a day till their polish gleams.
Words worth saying over and over,
Reassuringly, without tripping
Or getting out of sync. So sad

They merely tumble, rattling
Like empty beer cans
Crushed and rough-edged
That only wear and tear can tame.

(ii)

They only rattle rights and wrongs
Against the unyielding bars
Of unchallengeable conviction.
Do bile-bears peer out,
Simply assuming our cage
Is merely larger and greener
Than theirs? Do we, in caging them,
Ever realise their bars are our prison too?

ON THE EDGE

Time does its best and worst,
Slow as sloth, quick as lime:
Between the birth-scream
And the death-rattle
Only the humming spleen
Of the machine can
Measure presences learning
The sad beginning of the end,
Those infinite, confiscating definitives
Like David's loveless love for Saul.

DROWNING

Peering over the teetering edge
Of the war-time water tank,
Leaning into the reflection
With treacherous curiosity.
The abrupt fall, beckoned,
A flail un-stilling the pond.
Blankness. A forgotten gasp
In the upside-down world.
Plucked by the scruff, I spew
Chokes of weed-rotten water
And drink air …. having learned
To fear the drowned man.

OLD BRICKS

Water niggles its way into cracks, crevices,
The tiniest pores and pools there until the first frost,
Swelling and bloating into ice …
Ice that strains and stresses brickwork –
Like Sunday-best clothes tautening
At the seams – till it gives, yields, snaps, flakes.
The slightest flaw, blemish, widens,
Scooping out hollows where pigeons
Cling, sharpening beaks, trimming claws.
It does not take long to make a fine ruin
Our great-great-great-grandchildren
Will conjecture over.

THE AMMONITE

I was never meant to see the sunlight
But my spiral carapace survived
In the compressed sea-bed cemetery-silt,
And even the planet's shrugging
Tectonic drift that heaved me
Into this bright air. Look on me now,
In this work of polished marble,
And know that I have found
A kind of eternity that
You will eternally be denied.

THE FIG TREE

Shunned, perhaps still ashamed
Of the shame its leaves once hid,
It grows in the parched rubble
Of the toppling dry-stone wall
Behind the derelict mansion,
Oozing stickiness, ignored all year
Till the fruit, first hard
And green as walnuts,
Ripens, plump and splitting,
Inviting mouths and tongues to pry,
To savour the seed-gritty red flesh –
And perhaps recall
It was an apple started it.

ROADSIDE MADONNA WITH A BROKEN NOSE

These days, nobody bothers much any more
About this Madonna and her broken nose
Set in the last rickety bit of wall that once
Enclosed the manor house, itself now long gone.
She looks out over our rubbish bins today,

Her chipped nose turned up in apparent disgust.
Those folded hands never held a divine bambino,
And that mass-produced smile has become
A disgruntled grin. Soon, she will smirk over our
Discarded affluence, the gift-wrapped nonsense

We were fictitiously so pleased to receive
But only all too delighted to dispose of.
She has plastic flowers for company
And the empty remains of a shoddy,
Blood-red votary candle-holder.

The slotted box for odd coins underneath
Was thoroughly vandalised years ago.
The wind-flicked vines that will eventually
Reclaim this shrine have shrivelled for Winter.
It's cold and occasional passers-by
Have little time or inclination to stop
A second or two for thoughts of eternity.
While speeding cars brake hard
For the sudden junction hidden ahead,
Someone prayerlessly lets a bin lid slam.

FRONTIERS

Of course, our side is better.
Over there, they are uncouth,
Do things differently and worse.

Bridges we have built and destroyed,
Remnants of friendships and rivalries,
Hand-me-down loves and hatreds.

It hardly ever occurs to us at all
That walls keep as much together as apart:
Divisions seditiously unite.

AT THE END OF THE DAY

A dog-eared sky quibbles with day's end,
That hesitant transition from bickering light
Into dollops of darkness. The horizon's luminous
Rim dithers towards its imperceptible, invisible
Depletion as towns on the opposite shore
Illuminate for evening in a crowded loneliness
Of stolen hopes; this huddle of fears stirs an uneasy
Sense of coping with being unable to cope.
How much longer will the sleeping volcano slumber?

FRATERNISING WITH THE ENEMY
(Christmas in the Trenches 1914)

The big artillery fell strangely silent
As the machine guns' ragged babble
Imperceptibly faded away -
Even the snipers' rifles' cackle
Stuttered to an end. Someone sang
A carol echoed with yet more
From the other side. White flags
Welcomed an unofficial truce.
The braver men sauntered out
Into no-man's-land to swap fags
And grog. They kicked a ball about
And showed off their photos, discovering
That the enemy was not in front
But safe, far behind them.

THE REVOLT

There is fear on either side of the barricade.
A vociferous handful has faces if not hearts
In one or the other contention
Yet the mostly-silent or muttering rest –
Generally young, generally poor, all afraid,
Who all would rather be elsewhere –
Could cross the lines back and forth
Without making any noticeable difference
To the cohesion of opposites,
This division eternally uniting them.

SUBMARINE
"Engines off. We are going silent.
No smoking or talking."

Only the sonar pings

To the shudder

Of depth-charges

Like a stifled cough

Out there, above,

Below, around,

Suspended

Like a catch

Of cold-sea cod

Waiting to be

Trawled and gutted.

VULTURES

Menace, at noon,
Livid blue sky;
Obscene eyes rove
Shimmering landscapes.
Bones and batons thud,
Fall, in a far-off country,
Monotonously...

P.O.W.

The victory of survival
Is this lump of salt
I suck like a crow
Craven for carrion,
Dreaming of sugar.

Addicted, I lick
My own sweat.

STRATIGRAPHIES

Whatever is made
And what's undone,
Whatever's laid down
And then uplifted,
All that is hidden,
Submerged, eternal...

That sometimes make
Our empty souls
Tinkle: at times, emptiness
Is cumbersome.

We are interested
Only in frills,
The disposable
Side of life,

We realise things
Won't fit but still try
To shape them into
Something other than

Frivolous things that
Do not require
Too much thought
And next to no

Nothing. An edited
Version of the truth.
We share what's
In the middle

Feeling. We have
Come this far
So may as well
Traipse a few more

Dividing us, only
Nobody was climbing
The wall to get in.
Play safe: give up

Miles along this
Inclination towards
Nothingness, crossing
Secret borders

Gambits and trundle
Underarm wides.
There is no easy access
To other ways out.

CONVERSATION NEAR CALAIS

I was here during the war, you know, towards the end, of course.
I liked it here (all the shooting was over!) and have been coming
Back to this little village ever since. They know me here now,
In the hotel, trust me with their kids. I'm part of the family.
You won't believe it but this is my de-mob suit!
You'd never know it's forty years old. They made things properly then.
I get it out every August for two weeks. Brings back memories.
The wife hated it here the only time she came,
So I always popped over alone, after that first trip together.
I think she was jealous. They treat me well, here,
Not like at home where no one listens to me.
And, of course, now that she's gone, I could come
When I please but prefer August – there's more people, you see,
Makes it a holiday. I spend my days in the garden, evenings in the bar.
I enjoy travelling - though come to think of it,
This is the only place I've ever been to!
Naturally, I've learnt a bit of the lingo,
Bon jure, bon soir, se se bon, Bojollies, Borginyon, Coat dew Roane
And all that, so I can still enjoy my tipple: wine here, beer at home.
I could tell you a few stories about this place.
They modernised it a bit twenty years ago
But my room is always the same. French furniture of course.
Let me tell you a little secret: in my will I've asked to be buried here.
Yes!! Here! In Wissant! In my de-mob suit! What do you say about that!
Well, who's that coming in? I must say "bon evening" to him ...
Nice talking to you...

I was here during the war, you know, towards the end, of course....

CAUCHEMAR NEAR CALAIS

Him? That man over there?
He was *here during the war,*
Towards the end, of course,
As he always tells everyone.
You'd think he won it single-handed!
It's something *we* prefer to forget.
Life goes on, doesn't it?
He's turned up every year
Ever since in the same moth-balled
Pinstripe blue suit and books
Twelve months in advance
So we can't ever fob him off
That we are full.
Always the same room, though
He complained when we did it up.
His *dear departed wife* came once:
I think he bored her to death.

He never goes further astray
Than the garden and the bar,
Pretending in his awful French
To be the *oncle anglais*
Of our kids. He gets on their nerves
No end. Mine too, to be honest.
You'd think after all these years
He'd have picked up a bit more
Of the *local lingo* as he calls it.
Bojollies and Borginyon indeed!
And the poor sod wants to be
Buried here when he pops his clogs.
In that dreadful suit.
There's no accounting for taste.
C'est la vie and all that.

Well, enjoy your stay.
It was nice talking to you …

MOUNTAIN WIFE

I hate it up here,
I absolutely hate it.

I hate the seeping ooze
Of chill water
From grit-dirty snow
That spoils my shoes.

I hate my husband
And my kids for loving
What I try to understand
But can never love.

I hate all this hating.
God-above,
I could've loved them
More if only the city

Lights were closer
Than just a vision
Way below
Where my dad took me

Once or twice
For a treat
That still churns
My memories, my regrets.

IL COLLACCIO, UMBRIA

We have travelled wide and far
To see this moon peering
Between clouds the wind drives
Over immemorial mountains.

Distant lights make a claim
Of oneness with this place,
A tenacious, brief belonging
To a landscape that changes

Only on the surface, its roots
Vitally invisible, safe. The
Inkling that this might just be
Somewhere to come back to.

TRAVELLER

I am back in known territory
Where streets are reasonably chartered
And the signposts can be relied upon.
I spent years trying to fit jagged words
Into round and square holes,
Deburring one and the other, pointlessly
Seeking the perfect match,
The settled expression poising
What is said, what is heard,
In an acceptable equilibrium.
The lights are coming on again
And I'm finding my bearings once more.
I'm not sure where I have been
Or even where I am going –
May be it's the journey that counts,
The milestones we can list along the way.
Where we have been is of relative importance,
In any case, what matters most, perhaps,
Is the bag packed ready for another attempted journey.
Many people were met *en route*
And many came with us over long stretches
With advice and sometimes even deception.
We got lost, took wrong turnings
And found ourselves several times
Back at the starting point,
Confused by shifting perspectives
That may be coming to an end now.
Then again, perhaps not.
I suppose, all in all, we shall
Never know when it is over,
Since even the start took us unawares.

THE POISONER

After I got rid
Of my first wife
With arsenic in her soup,
The next one got

A taste of weed-killer
In a gin and tonic.
Naturally, I was forensically
Perfect. It was their

Fault, of course,
Eating and drinking
Like that, sluts to the end.
Missus number three

Has no idea at all
Her next dish
Might just contain
Saffron and cyanide.

I make such nice meals,
Such nice cocktails.

TRAVELS WITH DANTE

Was exile from Florence
Politics interfering with art
Or the other way round?
That as may be, you had friends
As keen to keep you at home
As enemies determined
To see you banished.

Yet, at least, you avoided
Loyal Socrates' poor fate
Proving then as now
That false accusers all too
Easily go scot-free:
Disproving presumed guilt shifts
The onus from defence
Of presumed innocence.
The slur and the smear
Are proof enough of culpability.

Well, you evidently packed your
Quills and parchments, ink,
Books and other essentials
And took your protruding
Lower lip to other horizons.

Some say your poetry
Would never have existed
Without such punishment –
Never to return home

On pain of death –
Even as you carried
On plotting and conspiring.

The enemies of your enemies welcomed you,
Some out of friendship and admiration,
Others for expediency. Dubious allegiances:
Scheming and intrigue are always rife
Yet this perhaps inspired your choice
Of guide around the Underworld.
Vergil, of course, had no idea of the destiny
You had in store for him – history doesn't
Always travel in straight lines. Companionship
At times can turn time's hourglass on its head.

I've been up and down this route
Many a time and seen the road-sign quote from
The Divine Comedy in huge lettering announcing the
"Ruins" –
The huge avalanche of rocks you would probably still
recognise.
You might even recall a church or two
And possibly the walled-in manor still nestled
In a gentle slope despite the new-fangled road and railway.
Less so the scruffy winter undergrowth –
Nature's ugly attempt to reclaim humanity's worse
And far more brutal ugliness: illegal rubbish tips,
Sewage treatment plant, derelict buildings
And industrial scum floating on streams that feed

The great river. Yet, these precariously-perched,
Tumbled stones still suggest some grandiose vision
Of your poet's journey on foot and horseback
Dragging your Florentine mission behind you
Always in your mind's eye. And thwarted love.

Sooner or later, we find out
Our handholds on life
Lose their grip (that perhaps
Was not all that firm in the first place).
Despondency chews what little time
We have and spits the mangled bits.
We are left with a little more slack
To take in, a little less hope.

Heroic vineyards clutch their way up
West-facing mountain slopes that once
Indifferently watched 800 invasions
Down this valley in 500 years
After the fall of Rome. The river, now,
Is crammed into its stationary bed,
Squeezed between cars and trains,
Unable to meander its way back and forth
Across the widening floor it eroded
Into home but no longer owns.

It's said you had mistresses, lovers
And even children on these travels.
There's the chestnut tree
You are supposed to have sat under
Near the great natural stone arch

And here's a genuine direct descendant
Running a wine-growing estate.

Light slashes its way through
Storm clouds stubbornly gathering
In the fast-approaching distance
As the train chugs me home.
I can't help wondering how exactly
Messer Alighieri travelled all this way himself:
Plodding horses pulling a plodding waggon
With a pack-mule for his manuscripts?
Servants? Family? Overnight stays in the inns
With cattle herders and brigands?
Sweaty stables and sweatier stable-boys?

Perhaps it was as well
They banished you
From all that factional bickering,
The money of politics, the politics
Of religion. Exile was supposed
To be punishment, like expulsion
From Eden into a hostile world.
We often need to move away
To get a closer look at what
Stirs or dulls our hearts,
Pinpoint what troubles the mind.
It also meant you could be
More explicit, more damning.
At last, you could do some
Of your own back-stabbing –
At a much safer distance.

LOE BAR, CORNWALL

In the bay of shipwrecks
The headlands open like arms
Welcoming the hemisphere-long Atlantic;
The gentle thrash of waves
On sand soothes and calms.

A tamed river spills out.
Blue sea and bluer sky seem
One stretch of immutable colour.
The hump of the bar holds back
Stilled freshwater were seagulls scream.

Unimportant hills unroll
Strangely to sea and lake.
Clumps of scrub and sea-thistle
Somehow keep their grip
In all the storms winter can make.

Storms that assaulted the place,
Heaving land one Mediaeval midnight
To block the estuary, turning safe
Anchorage to all-lost wreckage
With their Arctic might.

A hesitant equilibrium,
Its beauty wrought of violence.
Cruel oceans may come again
And set the river free,
Making some other excellence.

DEAD CALM

The ocean laps against the hull
Like a cat licking milk;
A sail flaps uselessly in the lull
Against a sky crinkled like silk.
Men amble and chat, or mull

Over empty pipes, the empty sea,
Thinking of a better elsewhere.
Someone swears and goes for a pee.
Captain furrows his fingers in prayer
And checks positions unnecessarily.

All of us have dead calm days
When the driving wind drops
To a weak breeze and then betrays
All will to move, when thoughts are slops
Simply for ignoring, like strays,

When the world is just an expanse
Of nothing and nothing can be done
To break the stultifying trance,
All's lost and nothing's to be won,
Life a caprice left to chance.

PRIMAL

The way the land lies
Or the wind scoots in off the sea,
Sea-birds balancing on the air
Or diving into shoals of sprat;
The way the clouds gather and disperse
Above us, struggling along the shingle;
The boom of surf crashing and scratching
At the shore; the smooth-backed,
Barley-bearing hills defying the wind,
And the salt, the trees born of gales and rock,
Crooked but strong-rooted:
A kind of going back to elements,
Sunlight, the moody sea green or blue,
Blue or grey the sharp air,
Stones in our shoes, sand, soil:
Fire in the remembering eye.

ONCE UPON A TIME

I'd rather not recall all this,
Now that the plain men have come
In their plainer uniforms with dull faces,
Turning our old freedom

Into something terribly obscene
From confession after confused confession.
You may know what I mean
About their icy obsession

With their own truth, their plan
And programme that never let me
Be a child, making me an old man
With only a bungled memory

Of love and innocence.
My stiff-aged bones suffer the cold,
The gross impertinence
Of an unlived life. All told,

They have taken it all, all,
Faceless in boots and spectacular
Berets, small minds walking exceedingly tall
Speaking a new, incomprehensible vernacular.

BEWILDERMENT

Someone always slinks away
Glibly from the growling crowd
Throwing stones at the chance victim,
Fumbling with non-distinctions.

Ignorance leers from smug corners,
The wreckage of progress
Succumbs to injustice;
By no means immune to our own poisons,

Strange beasts will graze our mutant pastures
After the birth-howl of doomed innocence -
The immaculately raped virgin
Whose suffering is analytically somewhere else.

Since it won't happen to them,
The queues gawp at death's circus,
Tidy and blameless, asking no questions.
Bewilderment is pain-killed, duplicitous.

REFUGEES

Fields grow weeds and men grow weary.
What crops there are, thrive to waste,
What is planted, putrefies.
The land returns to its harvest of stones,
Hard as the heart in its haste
To marry theory,
Match wrong truths with right lies.
A lost dog scratches itself and groans.

Life's an image in a telescopic sight:
Who shoots first, survives.
What is made, crumbles, is left to rot,
What the Earth has done, does, will do
Is too patient for our lives,
Too utterly slight,
Too long what is and what is not
For understanding transitory as Summer dew.

Smoke spirals upwards where the bombs sleaze
Their morning, moaning, mourning spree.
What was, tatters to rags.
Blossoms observe the boy become an orphan,
The terrified girl's looted virginity.
All the time, the refugees
Pack hopes in bags,
Anonymous as sardines in a can.

CROSSING BORDERS

Questing freedom is a prison.
The great tundra out there,
Under the best possible summer sun,
Crackles beyond the humming wires,
Dungeon-deep.

We know we are not, can not be free,
Our only choice above all a decision
Not to chose among the inescapable causes
Of our failure, escape
What cannot be escaped.

That ultimate abyss.
Not all pain makes us stoics.
What is desired and what is attained
Are never aligned, as we teeter
On the edge

Of the sublime, still seeking the physical route
To spirituality,
Mere components, well-thumbed documents,
Separating us from ourselves,
From this harnessed world …

That could otherwise be beautiful.

WIDOW

I make the most
Of their sympathy,
Their need to be seen
To be good and generous,
That inward compassion
That never looks beyond
All these masquerades.

They are only concerned
With what they think
They feel for me.

They do not know
How well I know them.
Their grief is griefless.

So I let them gawp
At my apparent distress,
Keep me company

And do my shopping,
Pay the fat-legged woman
To do my cleaning
And prepare my revenge
For those sons
Who still think
On occasional Sundays
There will be something
For them to fight about
After my vicious death:

It will all be theirs
To haggle and dispute.

I've already thrown the money
Of my love
Into the dustbin of life.

NOMADS

Tracks off into the sand define their progress.
    They came from nowhere and have nowhere to go.
    Replenished for another assault on the desert,
Their lengthening shadows recede into the Sun.
The oasis settles back on its heels in the shade,
    Clears its throat, and un-busies itself until the next time:
    Between then and now no-one cares or knows what happens to them.
Inattentively swishing the flies away,
The traders fix their eyes on the figures slowly moving on.
Once the wind has erased their footsteps,
    And their shapes have suffused into the Sun and sand,
Their memory merges with the heat, wavers momentarily,
        And is gone.

Their coming meant nothing, nor their going,
    Save a little profit, a glance at a different face,
    And some news from the north.

The Sun tries to burn itself out, ever vigilant,
Like a warder's eye glowering down on a makeshift world.

And they wander like lost philosophers,
Rough hands shading eyes squeezed to slits against the glare of the Sun
    And the wind that nonchalantly whips up sand in flurries,
        Dry in the backs of throats.

And they are made of sand, or seem to be.
Impenetrable faces, scoured to texture of rock,
Eyes forever attending the distance, or, perhaps, the future -
Who knows what they are thinking?
All seem old and tired
As if smarting yet under some age-old dream of slavers,
Those smash-and-grab raiders coming like locusts;
Ransacked of manhood they moved, though there was nowhere to hide,
And still they move,
Moving without ever arriving.

Four poles and a bit of canvas
Suffice at the day's zenith to ward off the scorching rays,
And at night to store a little warmth.
All they possess is easily packed on to irritable camels,
More readily moved than the men to display irked patience.

Life is an unending ritual;
A few goats at the end of forty years
Seems a poor return on a total investment.
Even at death there is no peace
As the Sun and wind, eternal enemies,
Pick bones clean.

THE GREAT DEPRESSION

Half the time, I'm not sure what's going on.
One minute I was bringing home my pay, regular,
Proud to drop it on the kitchen table
For the missus to divide up into neat little piles –
It's best to let the women do the sums, you know –
So much for the rent, the coal, the tab at the shop
And my beer money for the week; sometimes,
There were even a few coppers for the kids,
Something for the wife and the tin-box under the bed
For a rainy day or the trip to Rhyl.
The next thing I know, I'm out of the house
In the morning like a spare dinner
Because I got on our May's nerves something awful
Mithering at home all day…
I wasn't the only one, either.
We get together evenings on the corner
For a natter and a moan.
Then it got that even my kids cleared off
Out of my way and the wife'd get storming mad
If I had a beer before a bite of lunch.
I seemed just to grow into myself,
Nothing for it, I just couldn't care less.
I stopped going to the gates to get a job –
There's simply nowt going.
I miss the street coming to life in the mornings,
The lights coming on all up to the main road,

The noises: the kettle whistling on the hob,
Her wrapping my sandwiches
And giving me a peck on the cheek
To shoo me off since there was the washing
Or something else men weren't needed for.
It's all so damn quiet now.
We don't kiss much these days. She worries.
But it was grand those Saturdays,
All of us down the Crown,
Me having a pint or two more than usual
And May sitting pretty on a rum and black.
We sang like a congregation
Only it got bawdy and Rob's wife at the bar
Got all het up and shushing.
It was only a bit of a lark.
We'd have bread and dripping for supper,
The kids tucked up asleep,
And I'd slip my fingers under her blouse,
And she'd laugh and say "stop that",
But she didn't mean it
And we'd do it there in the kitchen
In front of the fire, the moon shining
Through the window.
And I did love her.
None of that now. Times aren't the same anymore.
Don't reckon they'll ever be the same.

MR. PIKE

I watch them watching me
And know they think I'm stupid.
I look at myself in the mirror
And see those lone-wolf eyes –
Watery, empty, distant -
Staring blankly back at me
And think I'm stupid myself
At times. At times,
Even I wonder why
I never say anything.
I stopped smiling years ago
Because my teeth are so bad.
Perhaps that's why I never talk.

On Friday nights,
With my pay in my pocket,
I treat myself to a pint,
Go home and shave my head and chin,
All over,
Like a caged animal
Stripping its own fur.
The stubble is back for Monday.
My monkey-hand feels it grow
Again all week

But I watch them.
Oh yes, I watch them.
My old mum always says
"You're such a watcher!"
And she always also says
"Tidy yourself up a bit,

There's always a nice girl
Looking for a man, you know!
Your Dad found me, bless him."

I never knew him
But I watch the others
On the shop floor
Where I clean up the swarf,
The office bloke
Chatting up the woman
Who works the lathe.
She's an old tart
Who wears too much make-up
And cheap scent.
He should know better.
I think his ties fart.

I'd love to tell him one day
What a prat he is
But I just nod
And order a bacon sandwich
Like the rest of them
For lunch that does me too for dinner.

I'd love to howl at the bastards,
Snarl on their stupidity,
Frighten the shit out of them one day.

They know my eyes prowl.
They trust my distrust.

I am their reliable mirror.

MICHELANGELO'S DAVID

Schoolgirls giggled
At the flaccid manhood,
Took photographs

And read descriptions
From the guide books
Far too loudly.

I remember walking
Up the aisle
Past half-carved prisoners

Breaking out
From their marble forms
Like the lava-casts

Of Pompeii
Coming to life again
Under the roof light shaping

The splay of flexed legs,
The relaxed arm set ready
To slay Goliath,

Your eyes focused
More on the calling
Than the deed.

No wonder Florence
Made such a festival
When this giant

Was first wheeled
Tottering from
Your workshop

Into the square
To inspire men
With his impassive glory.

CREATION

I am a stranger here,
Seeking uneasy affinity
With an unknown,
Different creation:

That ancestral womb
Where timeless air still
Timelessly stirs and smoothes
These pregnant mountains

Into hillocky roundness
Clumped with tussocks
Of grazing grass
Where a beech forest

Once obliterated
Every stone-outcropping
Horizon till men
Not my ancestors came

To clear pastures,
Fell trees for fuel,
For ships, for
Their homes, their tools.

It was a rape
You somehow survived

SMUGGLERS

We traipsed the mule tracks
With our contraband
Of salt and salt-fish
With a constant eye
On the weather –
Dark, wet, muzzled nights
Were always best
When lazy customs-men
Kept beside their fires
In stone-cold forts
Sipping grappa,
Smoking *our* tobacco!

They caught us, once or twice …
There was a bad wound,
Sometimes, at times
Even worse a death.

We and his wife
Had this headstone
Carved for our honest
Travelling companion
Placed where he fell.

It's still there, withered
With time, the flaky date
And name barely legible,
Telling the lie of our hardships.

The rest of us got away
And we still sold the salt.
Of course,
What else could we do?

EMIGRATING

We packed a few boxes
And then threw half it all away.
We had enough troubles
To be going on with.

We wrapped some
Thick-rind cheese that would
Last the journey, a lump of
Sweet ham and biscuit-bread,

In the poverty-cloth
No one would inspect.
We had enough coins over
In the bitter end

To pay the stone-man
Something to leave our mark
On a lettered plaque
Commemorating our names,

Our being here, once,
And our going away.

LOCAL SCENE

Imminent winter heaves
Grey clouds over
Low-slung hills
Ready to break
On splendid towers
As the rioting river
Swills past ancient arches
Silted up with refuse
Over stranded stones
Where shrill, degenerate
Seagulls splash
Their unforgivable, uninhabitable
Gluttony.

OVER THE SKIES TO SEE

That vague old woman
Reminisced about
Usual-enough comings and goings
And uncustomary things –
The coastline alight
With semaphore fires
For Napoleon,
A hanging or a fight –
That he focused on
Down Time's microscope
With equal propensity
Backwards and forwards
As far as the inkling
That eternity is fickle.

TRANSHUMANCE

We know Winter is over
When the beasts get restless
In their stalls: forage-bored,

They somehow always sniff
Fresh grass in the still-chilled
Air fluxing down from up there

Where we have to go
Every high-eternal Summer
For three months and more

To graze hopefully-fat pastures.
Between herdings and milkings,
We mend what storms broke

In our long absence, the stink
Of manure and making cheese
Deep even in our fingernails,

Wood-fires forever under the vats,
Despite the rock-cracking Sun,
We huddle round on sudden

Fog-cold nights. We only
Count the money in our purses
Once we've decked our stock

With ribbons for the mandolin-ed
Trip back to dark hearths
And another kind of solitude.